GIANMARIA

BUCCELLATI

© Assouline Publishing
601 West 26th Street, 18th floor
New York, NY 10001
USA
Tél.: 212 989-6810   Fax: 212 647-0005
www.assouline.com

ISBN : 2-84323-373-9

Translated from French by Tania Sutton

Color separation : GEGM (France)
Printing by Grafiche Milani (Italy)

GIANMARIA BUCCELLATI

VINCENT-EMMANUEL RAGOT

ASSOULINE

in the shadow of Napoleon's gaze, on the ground floor of the Hôtel du Rhin, it seems as though time has stood still. Hiding behind the arches of the Place Vendôme is one of the last remaining curiosity cabinets of the twenty-first century: Gianmaria Buccellati. Buccellati... the name alone conjures up images of a Renaissance artist.

The poetry in motion in the choice of precious materials : pink, gray or yellow gold embrace each other in the subtle weave of the engravings playing back to bewitching stones like fire opals, rare spinels, rose-cut diamonds...

Everything here is about the fine balance between shapes and colors. Each piece of jewelry is the reflection of strange links between different eras and different shapes. It is this magical alchemy that gives Buccellati its unique, instantly recognizable style.

1740. Milan. The first fine jeweler and goldsmith of the Buccellati family, Contardo Buccellati, opens his workshop on the Via degli Orafi (known as Via Orefici today), not far from the famous Il Duomo Cathedral. The Italian aristocracy and upper class come in droves to have pieces of jewelry and rare objects made in this small workshop which soon becomes known throughout Italy.

Throughout the seventeenth and eighteenth centuries, the Buccellati family discreetly continues the work and keeps Contardo's tradition alive.

It is not until the birth of Mario Buccellati in 1891, however, that the Buccellati style that we know today comes to life. As a child, Mario is fascinated by jewelry and precious objects and has a natural talent for drawing. Endowed with a natural curiosity and conscious of the fabulous historical heritage that Italy has to offer, he gets an apprenticeship with Beltrami and Besnati, important fine jewelers and goldsmiths of the time whose jewelry and artifacts can still be found in European museums and collections.

mario is attracted to all kinds of materials and stones. He does research into forgotten techniques from Ancient Greece or the Middle Ages, his favorite era being the Renaissance. At twenty-eight years old, with his experience at Beltrami and Besnati to fall back on, he opens his first workshop. When Beltrami retires at the end of World War I, Mario, his most able and willing student, takes his place at the helm of the business and renames it Buccellati.

In 1919, almost two hundred years after his ancestor Contardo, Mario Buccellati opens up his shop on Largo Santa Margherita, a stone's throw away from the Teatro alla Scala. The fact that the Scala is so close is not the only reason why Mario succeeds in artistic circles. Indeed, he soon proves himself an artist in his own right and a greatly talented goldsmith. Although the Art Nouveau movement is coming to an end and the Art Deco movement is just beginning, Mario Buccellati does not really pay attention to passing fashions. He does not just want to copy the jewelry of the Renaissance, but rather interpret it. Like an alchemist, he blends styles, precious metals, and stones. He mixes with pleasure engraving or chiseling techniques and from his craftsman's hands works of art are born. His interest for rich fabrics, precious damasks or Venetian lace bring him to create new techniques which will make gold and silver look like these rare materials.

Very quickly, Mario's workshop becomes the place where one must be seen. The big families of Milan, such as the Sforzas, the Borromées, the Viscontis meet there and make him their friend. Soon, painters and writers blend in with his elegant clients of the Italian aristocracy. People go there to find "superb fragments" of the history of art concentrated in the form of jewelry or precious artifacts. The aura of Mario Buccellati grows and grows and his friendship with the poet Gabriele d'Annunzio remains the most striking example of this.

d'Annunzio, the famous literary dandy, was fascinated by Mario's work to the point that he gave him the name "Prince of Goldsmiths." Everybody knows that this great poet was a lady's man and a generous one. Gabriele d'Annunzio showered luxurious presents on his numerous friends, male and female. The Buccellati family archives are full of drawings done for him by Mario and the correspondence that the two men wrote to each other. The creation of more than a thousand unique pieces of jewelry and artifacts made to order testify to seventeen years of loyal friendship. He would often give a poem written in his own hand to the Prince of Goldsmiths, intended for one of his many mistresses. One of Mario's engravers would then faithfully reproduce the poet's handwriting inside a box made of golf and precious stones. Mario, being the loyal friend that he was, had this "living poem" taken to the beautiful lady of d'Annunzio's choice.

But d'Annunzio also liked his friend to create very refined objects for his own use: cigarette holders, engraved boxes of gold and silver, rings, pocket watches. He was enthralled by the objects that his friend created for him. As this letter sent by d'Annunzio with a new order on December 11th 1922 shows:

"My dear friend Buccellati, you know only too well what a poor sinner I am, I cannot resist temptation."

It would seem that the poet had already made his own the aphorism of another famous dandy, Oscar Wilde, who once said "I can resist anything, except temptation."

The reputation, the unique know-how and especially the style of Buccellati will go beyond the Italian borders with amazing speed. Soon, the Royal families of Spain and Egypt ask Mario Buccellati to create their tiaras, necklaces and precious artifacts. The Pope and the great cardinals of Rome also order ornamental objects from him. His success is such that in 1925 he opens another shop on the famous Via Condotti in Rome. Just as in his shop in Milan, the shop in Rome attracts refined and intellectual clients whose admiration for the work of the craftsmen and Mario's genius knows no bounds. Four years later, he opens another shop in the beautiful town of Florence on the Via Tornabuoni. As well as being a great artist, Mario Buccellati is also an audacious entrepreneur. Up until the Second World War, he never stops developing his firm, training new craftsmen to master engraving and chiseling on gold or silver and the most delicate stone settings.

World War II bring to a halt 20 years of intense activity. The craftsmen are scattered all over Italy. But after the war, Mario is not discouraged. He wants to reunite his team of "golden hands" and so decides to go along Italy's highways and roads, looking for his best craftsmen. The goldsmiths have become farmers or mechanics. Mario and his young son Gianmaria use all their persuasive tactics to convince the "golden hands" to come back to the workshops in Milan so Mario's drawings can once again come to life.

In 1951, while Europe is trying to get over the war, Mario Buccellati decides to make his name in America. With the help of his eldest son, Luca, he opens a small shop on 51st Street in the heart of New York City. Again, the Buccellati magic seems to work. The Americans are fascinated by these pieces of jewelry and objects that seem to have come straight out of an Italian Renaissance painting from the Frick Collection. His humble shop soon becomes a cult place in the realm of luxury goods.

The shop is tastefully decorated by Mario and the Buccellati family. He is the first Italian jeweler to open a shop on the prestigious 5th Avenue.

Mario, who sees the company getting bigger, gives his sons more and more responsibilities. They all work in the company, except for Giorgio, who becomes an eminent archeologist. Luca supervises the work done in New York. Federico runs the shops in

Rome and Florence. Lorenzo looks after the administration and the management of all the activities of the company. Only Gianmaria follows directly in the footsteps of his father, helping him with the design and the production of pieces of jewelry and gold.

In 1965, Mario passes away, leaving his sons a fabulous artistic heritage and the greatest wealth of all, the unique expertise of a hundred craftsmen: engravers, stone setters enamellers and lapidaries. Each of the Buccellati sons has his own vision of this wonderful heritage that the "Prince of Goldsmiths" has left them. Lorenzo and Federico decide to keep only the Italian shops, thus leaving to Luca and Gianmaria the development of the Buccellati name in the United States and around the world. The fact that the sons' paths separate enables Gianmaria to demonstrate his creative talents, and shows that he is an audacious and visionary businessman.

from an early age, Gianmaria followed in his father's footsteps and learned to follow all the different stages in the creation of a piece of fine jewelry with patience and humility. He learned all the different techniques by heart: the unique Buccellati engraving, stone setting, the choice of metals and stones.

Although his father was aware of his son's potential, he insisted on teaching all the aspects of the trade and made him start as a simple apprentice working on menial tasks in the workshops, all the while dreaming of incredible jewels.

Gianmaria likes to say that it is the craftsmen who taught him all he knows. With their precious advice and the help of his father, he was soon able to exploit his artistic talent.

After all, he is his father's son. Indeed, just like him, he had a natural thirst for knowledge: architecture, decorative arts and history. Everything interested him. He learned to draw quickly, mastering the strokes that with time become more and more precise.

His love for the eighteenth century in France made him more inclined to draw sumptuous finery in the style of those that Madame du Barry liked to wear. He also admired the great Parisian goldsmiths of the time like François-Thomas Germain, whom Voltaire called "the Divine Hand", and loved to develop ideas based on the wonderful shapes and swirls of the Regency.

When at long last Mario finally decided to hand over the reins of the Milan business to his son (who was just nineteen) Gianmaria discovers with pleasure the clientele of the Buccellati House. The important Milanese families had no problem at all in trusting this mature young man whose passion seemed to know no bounds. The meetings with his clients proved to be primordial in helping him to learn the ropes at the head of a business and he never tired of seeing his family's creations adorn the most beautiful women in Europe! He also discovered that the very feminine aspect and the delicate feel of the Buccellati work were excellent ways to "charm" his beautiful clients.

Soon, he began to share the management and production of the workshops with his father. With the opening of the shop in New York, and then other sale points in the USA, Gianmaria often had to supervise the work done in the workshops during his father's absence. During this time, he creates passionate bonds with his craftsmen, with whom he is demanding, but fair.

The "Golden Hands" had found a new master, one worthy enough to carry the Buccellati name into the future.

When his father dies, Gianmaria is only thirty-six years old, but already has more than twenty years experience behind him in the fine jewelry and goldsmith trade. He knows that the unique style and the high quality demanded in the creation of their objects are incredible assets in the closed circles of fine jewelry. The success of their creations among the international jet set remains the most obvious reflection of the place that Mario Buccellati made for himself in such a short time. Gianmaria Buccellati and his brother Luca have the same vision: to make Buccellati an international name by opening new sale points in the most prestigious places around the globe.

g ianmaria Buccellati takes on the management of the workshops, as well the creative part of the company. He designs, follows up and controls every piece of gold and silver that leaves the workshop. Luca, meanwhile, works on developing the business all over the United States. Over the next few years, Buccellati silverware becomes one of the name's biggest successes in the US. In 1968, the final separation from Lorenzo and Federico, who only want to stay in Italy, pushes Gianmaria Buccellati to reunite all his father's craftsmen to create a new company in the center of Milan.

In 1970, this audacious creator seems to be afraid of nothing. Gianmaria Buccellati decides to be the first Italian fine jeweler to create a business in Hong Kong, at the heart of the prestigious company Lane Crawford, as his father before him had in New York. Then, in 1972, with the help of the famous Japanese company,

WAKO Stores, Buccellati puts its name on the maps of Tokyo, Osaka and Nagoya. His Asian clients are enchanted by the fine jewelry of the Milanese goldsmith. The floral theme, which is especially close to the Buccellati family's heart, proves to be equally popular here. Both the leaves and flowers, which are recurrent in the Buccellati style, correspond perfectly to Asian aesthetics.

but the biggest adventure is yet to come. Riding the wave of the success acquired in the USA, Hong Kong and Japan, Gianmaria Buccellati dreams of coming back to redevelop his business in Europe. He sets his sites on Paris's mythical Place Vendôme, "the most beautiful showcase in the world," which at this time, in 1979, displays the biggest names in French jewelry: Boucheron, Chaumet, Mauboussin, Van Cleef & Arpels. This famous square — an architectural marvel designed by Jules Hardouin-Mansart — is a unique symbol in the world of French luxury. Gianmaria dreamt of setting up the family name in this hallowed place just as his father did before him. It is because of an extraordinary coincidence that Gianmaria becomes the first Italian jeweler to set up his business in the temple of French fine jewelry: a friend tells him that the ground-floor of the Hôtel du Rhin will be put up for bidding in a candle auction. Knowing nothing about this typically French practice, but dreaming already of this superb site, he leaves Milan for Paris on the spot. Gianmaria falls in love with this private mansion where Brillat-Savarin lived and sees this detail as a good omen for the fine gourmet that he is. A few weeks later the auction candle goes out, and Gianmaria wins the bid for Number 4 Place Vendôme.

The father's dream has come true through the son, as if the spirit of Mario had himself blown the candle out.

After more than nine months of work on the site, Gianmaria Buccellati restores this unique spot to its 18th century style that is so dear to him, as if, by doing so, he is paying a respectful tribute to French arts.

Another wonderful surprise: Gianmaria and his interior decorator discover a part of the sumptuous woodwork of the private mansion of "La Guimard", a famous dancer immortalized by the painter Fragonard. The workshops of the Faubourg Saint-Antoine restore with passion and dedication, this superb woodwork and transform the 2,800 square feet of 4 Place Vendôme into a splendid suite worthy of the Regency.

On December 10th 1979, all the members of the Buccellati family unite to inaugurate with rightful pride this sumptuous site, a site that Gianmaria will from then on call "the crown of his kingdom."

To celebrate, elegant party at the Ritz, dinner Chez Maxim's and Anouk Aimée, one of the most moving French actresses, to accompany Gianmaria, the artist and his muse. Thus did Gianmaria Buccellati enter the magical, cocooned world of the Place Vendôme.

The incomparable prestige of this Parisian Square enables the Buccellati family to attract an international clientele and enhance the reputation of the company. With the help of his wife Rosie, his daughter Maria Cristina and his sons Andrea and Gino, he multiplies the projects to develop the company. Mario Buccellati II (Luca's son) supervises the business in the United States.

The opening of new shops enables the company to expand even more, and today, the workshops of Milan and Bologna employ more than 600 craftsmen.

The conception and creation have never suffered from the impressive development of the company. Gianmaria and his son Andrea still draw and design all of the fine jewelry and artifacts.

The most striking example of the Buccellati's love of tradition is that the most qualified craftsmen come and present their work to Gianmaria and Andrea every Friday, pulling out paperbags filled with rings, necklaces and bracelets on to the desks of father and son.

In 2000, a touching tribute is paid to the Buccellati family and the hundreds of craftsmen who work for them at the Smithsonian Institute in Washington.

t he museum, which holds one of the most beautiful stones in the world in its permanent collection, the blue Hope diamond, had never before honored a fine jeweler — living or dead — for his work.

The works of Mario Buccellati, such as the silver objects created for Gabriele d'Annunzio, were presented, along with a collection of very beautiful pieces of jewelry created by Gianmaria over more than thirty years of work and belonging mostly to private collectors. The extraordinary pieces of the personal Buccellati collection, such as cut rock crystal glasses mounted on gold and ruby stems, left their Milanese bank safes for the first time. This exhibition was a great success in all the American towns in which it was shown.

2002 represents an important year for Gianmaria, as it marks his arrival in the very restricted circle of Swiss clockmakers, with the presentation of his new collection of more than four hundred pieces in Geneva. The collection includes dress watches in engraved gold with a dazzling cobbling effect (created by using pink diamonds or rubies), and a bracelet in engraved gold, then covered with leather — a selfish but divine luxury!

Golden lace, cascades of rare stones, the mysterious shimmer given off by precious metals — these are the results of almost two hundred years of jewelry creation, the assertion of a style that is timeless and of a very unique expertise.

Buccellati jewelry is not a slave to any fashion. It transcends time and place: that's the reason why its beauty cannot — and will not — be tarnished...

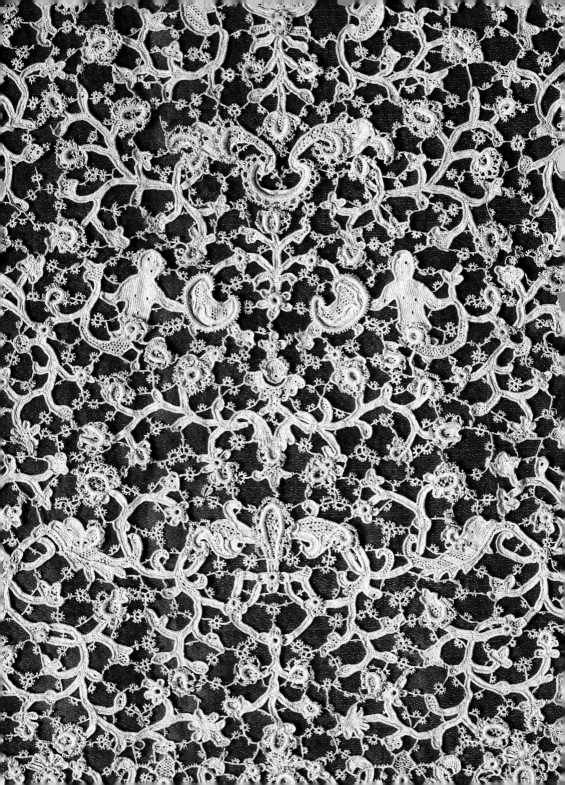

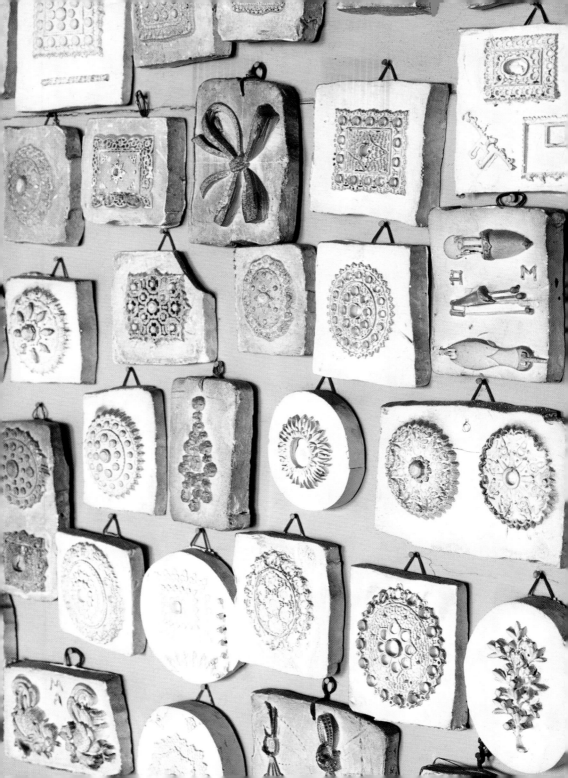

ti manderò molto di
più prima del 20 ottobre.

Grazie.
Lavoro. Verrò a Milano
presto. Son certo che il Maestro
paragon Coppella" fa sempre
nuovi miracoli di gemme
d'oro.
Arrivederci.

Gabriele d'Annunzio

Il Vittoriale: 2 ottobre 1924

Chronology

1740: Contardo Buccellati opens the first fine jewelry and goldsmith's workshop in Milan.

1891: Birth of Mario Buccellati in Milan.

1919: Mario Buccellati opens his first shop on Largo Santa Margherita in Milan.

1923: Gabriele d'Annunzio orders a chain necklace composed of rubies and a yellow beryl that he offers to the famous actress Eleanora Duse.

1924: Opening of the shop in Rome on the famous Via Condotti.

1930: Opening of the shop in Florence on the Via Tornabuoni.

1945: Mario Buccellati makes his way around Italy looking for his craftsmen.

1951: Opening of the first shop in New York on 51st Street with the help of Luca Buccellati.

1954: Opening of the prestigious shop on New York's 5th Avenue.

1965: Death of Mario Buccellati in Milan.

1966: Gianmaria Buccellati takes over the management of the workshops.

1968: Business separation from his two brothers, Lorenzo and Federico.

1970: Opening of the shop in Hong Kong with Lane Crawford.

1971: Gianmaria opens his first shop in the hotel "Cala di Volpe" on the "Costa Smeralda" in Sardinia.

1972: Signing of the sales contract with WAKO Stores which covers the distribution of Buccellati jewelry in Japan. The jewelry is launched simultaneously in Tokyo, Osaka and Nagoya.

1973: With a group of fellow jewelers, Gianmaria Buccellati founds the "Italian Gemology Institute" of which he has been the president since its creation.

1979: Opening of the Place Vendôme shop, thus asserting the international reputation of the Buccellati name alongside the most prestigious names in the world of fine jewelry. The Italian president gives him the title of "Cavaliere di Gran Croce al merito della Repubblica" (Knight of the Great Cross and the national Order of Merit).

1981: Opening of a sale point in Porto Cervo, Sardinia, on the Piazzetta degli Archi.

1982: Opening of a shop on the Calata Mazzini in Portoferraio, on the Island of Elbe.

The arches of the superb front of the Hôtel du Rhin, 4 Place Vendôme. © Collection Gianmaria Buccellati, Milan.

1983: Opening of a "Gianmaria Buccellati" shop, Via Montenapoleone, on the Piazzetta La pyramide in Milan.

1989: Gianmaria opens a new shop in Beverly Hills at the Beverly Wiltshire Hotel.

1995: Opening of shops in Venice and Capri.

1999: The millennium set, which comprises a necklace and a pair of earrings worked in honeycombed gold and set with more than 65 carats of diamonds, is finished after more than two years work.
The composer Giovanni Sollima present the world premiere performances of *Viaggio in Italia* at the Carnegie Hall in New York, deditated to Gianmaria Buccellati ,as a tribute for all his musical patronnage .

2000: The "Gianmaria Buccellati" exhibition at the Smithsonian Institute in Washington, DC. This exhibition traces the careers of Mario and Gianmaria Buccellati. The exhibition travels throughout the United States.

2001: First "Gianmaria Buccellati" world show in Geneva, where the company made a startling debut in the clock-making world.

2002: 2002 Opening of a new shop in Miami.
The "Diamonds" exhibition representing the most beautiful creations in diamonds ever made at Scuderie del Quirinale in Rome.

"The Pleasure Chalice", a sumptuous cup in rock crystal, mounted on a stem in engraved gold lace and embellished with rubies (9.92 cts) and emeralds (5.06 cts). © Gianmaria Buccellati, Milan. Private collection.

Pill box in engraved silver, which belonged to Gabriele d'Annunzio. On the lid, we can read the following words: "I have received much more than I have ever given." Mario Buccellati. © Collection Gianmaria Buccellati, Milan.
Letter from Gabriele d'Annunzio to the "Prince of Goldsmiths" and two cigarette holders in engraved silver. Mario Buccellati, 1934. © Collection Gianmaria Buccellati, Milan.

Large drop earring in white and yellow gold, set with diamonds (5.4 cts) and a pear emerald (2.32 cts). © Collection Gianmaria Buccellati, Milan.
Large drop earring in white and yellow gold set with diamonds and rose-cut diamonds (3.65 cts). © Collection Gianmaria Buccellati, Milan.

"Tulle" brooch in yellow or white gold. Collection Gianmaria Buccellati, Milan.
"Tulle" necklace. A very delicate collarette necklace in honeycomb engraved gold, set with diamonds and drops encrusted with rubies (17.85 cts).
"Tulle" brooch set with emeralds and diamonds embellished with a diamond center. © Photo by Anita Calero / Collection Gianmaria Buccellati, Milan.

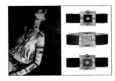

"Sunflower" brooch with petals in yellow engraved gold set with diamonds and embellished with a smoked quartz cabochon. © Photo Oliver Spies for *Air France Madame* / Collection Gianmaria Buccellati, Milan.
The new "Agalmachron" collection of watches in engraved gold. Strap in gold covered with leather, enamel or diamond and black diamond face. © Collection Gianmaria Buccellati, Milan.

"Rouche" necklace in fine white and yellow gold lace set with diamonds (207 diamonds, 7.29 cts). © Photo Isabelle Bonjean / Gianmaria Buccellati, Milan.
Necklace in fine white and yellow gold lace set with diamonds (380 diamonds, 24 cts) and a cabochon pear emerald (29.31 cts). © Gianmaria Buccellati, Milan.

Three bracelets, a pair of earrings and a ring in engraved gold set with diamonds. © Gianmaria Buccellati, Milan.

The new "Eliochron" collection of watches in engraved gold. Strap in gold covered with leather, enamel or diamond face. Gianmaria Buccellati, Milan.

The author is especially thankful to Martine Assouline and her team.
The author and publisher express their thanks to everyone in the Buccellati family, and
in particular Maria Cristina and Gianmaria Buccellati, and all of the employees in the
studios and offices in Milan, Conde Nast, Editions Laurent Jalou, Isabelle Bonjean,
Anita Calero, Patricia Campagne, Ralph Delval, Léna Kersuzan, Émily Minchella,
Franceline Prat, Olivier Spies, Ferdinand Ripoll, Paul Steinit and Tania Sutton.